Mealfest

The Secret, Never Before Seen, Management Formula for Restaurants in an Appetizing Self-Help Book

By

George S. Hearing

authorHOUSE™

1663 LIBERTY DRIVE, SUITE 200
BLOOMINGTON, INDIANA 47403
(800) 839-8640
WWW.AUTHORHOUSE.COM

This book is a work of non-fiction. Unless otherwise noted, the author and the publisher make no explicit guarantees as to the accuracy of the information contained in this book and in some cases, names of people and places have been altered to protect their privacy.

© 2005 George S. Hearing. All Rights Reserved.

No part of this book may be reproduced, stored in a retrieval system, or transmitted by any means without the written permission of the author.

First published by AuthorHouse 02/25/05

ISBN: 1-4208-1562-8 (sc)

Printed in the United States of America
Bloomington, Indiana

This book is printed on acid-free paper.

DEDICATION

I want to dedicate this work to my loving wife, Tracy, my children, Allison and Joshua, to my mother-in-law who has always encouraged me to write, and to my mother who always has encouraged me in *everything*.

ACKNOWLEDGEMENTS

In high school, I always thought it a tedious task to "journal" my thoughts and reflections on things around me. The head of the English Department at Christ school, the Episcopal Boarding School I attended in Arden North Carolina, Reed Finley, must have thought it tedious countering sophomoric (although it had to be moronic) arguments as to why it was not productive to do journals. I must acknowledge now, his wisdom, although I may not have thought so then, is "Big." His influence was similar to his stature and his presence in the lives of those young men.

I would be remiss in not acknowledging the impetus for the creation of this work. I heard an explanation about how to organize thoughts into a book in May of 2002, and I started an outline and moved from there to piece together *Mealfest*. Thanks go to Dave Ramsey for sharing, caring and serving in the way he does on the radio everyday. He is helpful to many and his inspiration is beyond words. He has written several self-help (the genre title does not do the work justice) books and steers a show daily to millions of listeners.

Finally, "cousin Doug" encouraged me with his presence and energy. Doug Litteral is the author of several books on "MANuals" for life that should be read by all. His persistent accountability practices and insights on getting people to make a difference are keen.

It is also dedicated to the readers.
It must be remembered that we work to exist, not
exist to work; we work to grow, not grow to work;
and we work to prosper, not prosper to work.
Often, all of us busying ourselves with the task at
hand
do not see the goal that we are striving for. Setting
your sights on a
target is always a must. I am not so presumptuous as
to tell you
the goal:
you must set the goal
and strive for it relentlessly.

CONTACT INFORMATION
georgehearing@yahoo.com

George S. Hearing
P.O. Box 412
Cowan, TN 37318

x

TABLE OF CONTENTS

DEDICATION v

ACKNOWLEDGEMENTS vii

PREFACE xiii

CHAPTER 1 EMPLOYEES… CAN'T LIVE WITH 'EM, CAN'T LIVE WITHOUT 'EM… 1

CHAPTER 2 SCHEDULES The Schedule is never done. 11

CHAPTER 3 SITUATIONS Situational Management 19

CHAPTER 4 TIME ROBBERS Plan to be Interrupted. 27

CHAPTER 5 ACHIEVEMENT "Work For Food" .. 33

CHAPTER 6 DEPENDABILITY, DISCIPLINE, AND DEVELOPMENT Going in the right direction develops you and others 41

CHAPTER 7 COMPETITION Who's breathing down your neck? 51

CHAPTER 8 CONSISTENCY Do your job the same way, the right way, everyday. 59

CHAPTER 9 INTERVIEWING 67

CHAPTER 10 MUSINGS 77

CHAPTER 11 FORMULA FOR ACHIEVEMENT RISE to the next level. 85

CHAPTER 12 THE LAST CHAPTER: SATISFACTION 91

E(exist) G(grow) P(prosper) List 99

PREFACE

<u>MEALFEST:</u>
<u>The Secret, Never Before Seen, Management Formula</u>
<u>For</u>
<u>Restaurants in a</u>
<u>Appetizing Self-Help Book</u>

What started as an appetizer quickly became
a seven course meal that has me eagerly anticipating
the dessert menu.

I started working in a restaurant, not knowing that I would spend my life doing it, when I was 12 years old. The name of the restaurant was *The New Orleans Shrimp House*.

It was an appropriate name since it was in an old house. The downstairs was used for the restaurant and the upstairs (an attic) was barely big enough for a cot - one which I used when it was too late for me to work to sleep on while I waited for my brother and mother to finish their duties so we could go home.

The old house was two blocks from Tampa Bay where one could hear the ships' bells tolling and the dinghies bringing in their catches of the day.

The sea spray aroma and the cool, evening breeze wafted across the back deck of the *New Orleans Shrimp House* everyday. The fragrance of the outside air and the sounds of glasses and mugs dinging together figuratively took me to taverns the world over. These images lifted this writer to thoughts of exotic getaways and exciting get-togethers.

Inside, dining rooms teemed with personality of bygone days. The dishes were varied; hardly any two were part of the same set. The interior was small, lending itself well to intimate gatherings. A festive atmosphere abounded for all of the patrons as well as the crew who served them.

The hustle-bustle of the city was in the distant. This gentle setting offered a brief sojourn from the busy city goings-on that dominated so much of peoples' days.

This respite from the hectic schedules of people's lives is something I have long tried to duplicate in the different operations I have been a part of.

The dishwashing job I had was not mine for long. However, I reminisce about that seaside setting each and every time I enter into a task in the many dish rooms I have been in since. I strain to hear the tolling of ships, the waves beating on the sea walls and the aroma of the bay.

I worked in dozens of places over the next many years: different professions but many were restaurants/fast feeders.

I finished college and worked two years as an assistant director of admissions, a job where I learned interview skills as well as public speaking polish, and then back to the restaurant business I went.

I went to a small but growing company. I parlayed my limited supervisory experience (that which I gained when I was charged with scheduling, and directing about twelve different "work-study" students at the college) into a restaurant management position.

SOCIETY TRENDS

During the next two decades, many changes occurred in the world. We as a society, probably in large part due to two income families and limited time at home for many families, became so much of an "eating-out" or restaurant society, that many companies grew and flourished building many locations.

To some Ray Croc's sage words "saturation is for sponges" seemed to say "build on, there is no end to this boon". Now there are operators who are in this business with the sole purpose of going through the motions thinking that is all it takes. The business has been kind to some, and abhorrent to others. We must turn the temperature up or down ourselves: we tell the oven to cook, it doesn't tell us! McDonald's and other similar success stories made it and keep making it not just because of who they are, but because they prove a system works over and over again each day.

Many factors are involved in "making it happen" everyday. I have started out many a day not knowing which direction I would end up going with my operation: up or down, sideways or falling like a bad soufflé'!

We desire what we need but we do not always need what we desire.

If we are going to eat out, and spend good money to do so, then we want it to be as good as possible for the money we spend. We do not know exactly where we will go all of the time, but we are moving toward having the ability to be more selective in where we dine anywhere. We, as a society (in disposable income ability), are able and willing to choose dining places based on the quality *and* availability, as opposed to, just location. Our entertainment and eating out merge into "eat-a-tainment."

A good dining *experience*, in a raw sense, is not always necessary anymore because we as a society accept that service can be hit or miss, at any price, and at any place. Restaurant eaters are numb to the bad experiences and come in to restaurants not expecting any certain type of service, but just to eat. There are too many "low-standard" eating establishments. Good quality food and service is suspect, at the least, and occasionally non-existent at most places at any time.

Now, some restaurateurs would relish (good food term) the opportunity to serve folks that just want to eat and are innocuous to the quality of service. The proprietors of such places just hope that the experiences are not so bad that they will not return. Repeat business is always the goal and is paramount to survival.

Of course, restaurants that do not give attention to bad service, purely and simply, will not survive, because patrons are not totally innocuous to bad service yet. People are just not as surprised as in the past with bad service.

Twenty Years of Daytimer Notes, aka, Research

My research for this book has been keeping my eyes open during my restaurant career. I have used "daytimers" and written many things down through the years that I have heard from many different people from many different walks of life.

Many of the musings or thoughts that have flowed through my mind due to influences from many sources have been sustenance that has enriched, filled and nourished a career.

In the Oxford English dictionary, definitions are listed for many, almost all, known words. They are cited there with references as to where they were used in literature. They are not only defined, per se, but also referred to in their uses throughout literature.

In a sense, everything and everyone is defined this way. We are the sum of our experiences just as the definitions of words are their uses in the context of the printed literary sources.

CAN BE DONE BY ALL

This book is not about rocket science or anything that cannot be done by any one. It is a book of rambling ruminations regarding repasts! ("Always alliteration" is my motto!) Learning from stories is the best way to benefit from mistakes that anyone has made.

The many quotes that are used should be thought provoking that ultimately lead to better problem solving. After all, this is the only planet that we live on and all those who came before us lived, succeeded, tried and failed just as we have and just as we have seen many others attempt to do in our surroundings. Opinions are meant to motivate and inspire as well as, as often as is possible, educate and inform.

I would contend that people who have obtained greatness have borne the mantle of their status reluctantly, and very often, abhorred the function of having to share their story of how they achieved greatness. But, they go on and relate to others out of a sense of responsibility and feeling that they abhor ineptitude even more than ignorance.

I have witnessed many things that I do not care to share, and I feel that what I have shared here will help managers in restaurant operations in some way. I feel that being informed is the best approach to doing something or anything in this world.

WE ARE ALL IN THE ARENA

The credit belongs to the man who is actually in the <u>arena</u>; whose face is marred by dust and sweat and blood; who strives valiantly; who errs and comes short again and again; who knows the great enthusiasms, the great devotions, and spends himself in a worthy cause; who at best knows in the end the triumph of high achievement; and who at worst, if he fails, at least he fails while daring greatly.

-Theodore Roosevelt

So often we put down the lifestyle that we do not have without examining what we have and what others have. We seem to think that one way of doing something (i.e., making a living) is hard and another is not. We view anything and everything as one extreme or the other, as good or bad, no in between. The "efforts", (the "valiant striving") are due some recognition for what it does in the ebb and flow of all of our daily routines.

Looking to others to learn how to deal with situations is one of the best ways to approach problem solving. Whenever we excel in something, we are raising the standard in the "<u>arena</u> of quality"; therefore, we are requiring our competition to do a better job in order to compete with us.

If you make your competition better, then you are making yourself better because you must succeed "better" than your competition in order to keep succeeding. That's a mouthful… but this book will expound on that and explain what it all means in the forum of the restaurant environment.

Addressed are the characteristics of a successful and fulfilling career. It is instruction on survival and an opinion on achieving even more: true satisfaction. If this is your desire, read on because the recipe for fulfillment is on the ensuing pages.

CHAPTER 1
EMPLOYEES...
CAN'T LIVE WITH 'EM, CAN'T LIVE WITHOUT 'EM...

INCESSANT TURNOVER

One of the best ways to lose good employees is to keep bad ones.

So often we do the best that we can do and it is not the best that can be done in an ideal situation. Utopia is a fictional place, that is true, and utopian type performance is very rare if existent at all. The growing number of restaurant seats out there is requiring managers to find more and more people with the necessary experience to achieve the job required.

Not enough people have the necessary experience because there are so many restaurants that workers can come into, train, then leave to go the restaurant next door for a quarter more an hour. They leave *literally* days after getting trained because some one tried to actually *make* them do their tasks. Progressive discipline has to be more instructional than critical because employees are planning on working many jobs.

OWNERSHIP vs. CLOCK-WATCHERS

Many workers fall into two categories: ownership mentality and clock-watcher mentality. Those with the ownership mentality appear at work in an almost ethereal sense, just when you need them most. They jump into action in the middle of situations and try their hardest to solve the immediate crisis at hand.

On the other side of the spectrum is the "clock-watcher". They are the ones who walk in at the last minute, not ready to clock in until their allotted time, no sooner, no matter what the crew already on duty is experiencing. And "don't expect me to stay any later than my scheduled time out" is always their motto.

The "clock-watchers" and the "owners" are both necessary to have on hand to do the job. Self-motivators, self-employed individuals, and those with the ownership mentality have the drive it takes to succeed. He or she is the one person who can make a difference in their own employment future. No one can give you drive and determination.

Identifying the drive in individuals can help you develop it in your employees. It is certain that those with this drive will venture out on their own or move on from the ranks of the mediocre, mundane task-doers they are in now. But, while they are in your employ, you can rest as much responsibility on that "owner" as he or she will tolerate and grow your own operation immensely.

A young man walked into my restaurant looking for a job at sixteen years old. He struck me as a man at his word when I asked him if he was ready to start working right away and he answered, "I need to get in the proper uniform and can be back in one hour."

He was back in less than one hour. He worked with me in several different positions over the next four years. He always wanted to learn more and put himself in a better money making position. He now owns his own successful business in the same town.

You can rest assured this person plotted his own future as the operator of his own destiny unlike the "clock-watcher". The "clock-watchers" will stick to a job and not veer from the task at hand, as long as it is in their allotted time, no more, no less. Everyone has a hold on his own employment destiny.

It has been said that 18 year olds in the nineties will change jobs eight times before they retire. The tougher times that we as an economy have experienced in this young century will teach us all something that we haven't had to learn in a long time: a job is a valuable thing and we should keep it and cultivate it into something that is desirable and worth keeping.

So many people "job-hop" that we know that positions will get filled quickly. We as an industry do a disservice to the whole industry by snapping up people just as they quit another without notice.

One now amusing incident that occurred in one of my operations is a good example of this. A dishwasher felt overwhelmed during a very busy breakfast shift: he was up to his elbows in "egg plates". *Anyone* who has washed breakfast dishes knows how hard "egg plates" are to clean!

The young man obviously had a dilemma. He did not want to do this anymore, yet he did not want to just walk-out. He solved his dilemma by going into the lobby and calling the store office phone from the lobby payphone. He wanted to let us know he wouldn't be working there anymore. How efficient is that, calling and quitting before getting out the door!

EMPLOYEES IN TUNE and GUEST RETENTION

Managers fear that the motives and motivation of some of the subordinates are selfishly shallow. When you are endeavoring to make income by selling your product, be it food or service in a restaurant, the employee who wants to gain income should jump at the opportunity to do so as much as possible.

I have always taught that one should serve each and every table individually and we would succeed in the restaurant we were working in by taking care of every single table that walked into our restaurant. Each individual table would not in itself be a great deal of profit to the bottom line. It would not even cause us much economic loss if we did not get the revenue from that guest that "walks out" because he/she did not get served quickly, or served at all, or not well enough, etc.

But, return visits are the key to any operation and repeat business should always be on the forefront of our minds while we are in the restaurant working. Always take care of guests' needs first, then all other tasks, questions, comments, etc.

"Can you take this table?"

This is a phrase that host/seating staff will ask when it is busy or picking up fast. When it happens, the host/hostess is looking to get some guests in a seat because they have waited or seem to be in a hurry and there are empty tables and they are pressuring that door staff person to get them in one of them.

The server is busy and usually the door person knows who his/her strong servers are and goes to one of them (because if you want something done, get a busy person to do it!)

One thing to remember when in this business is that we must provide the service we are asking people to pay for. The quickest way to fail is to fall short of the value of the experience.

Whenever you hear these words, and a hesitated answer, then you know you should intervene. Other servers are around and won't jump in to help, unless you have staff members who are "in tune." They are in tune with growing your/their business because they know that each guest that walks into the building is valuable.

It only takes a moment and (therefore a very small amount of monetary investment) to greet and set the meal experience up for a guest that has just been seated either in a closed section or just where someone else has been seated very recently.

The "in tune" employee will be there instantly and with a pleasant demeanor to welcome that guest into the environment. Those employees who just want to do their part and get out when it is time to leave, they would avoid/ignore that guest.

So many times in the past I have wanted to stop reality and time and just say to that employee (the "clock-watcher"), just how do you think that the money is made to pay you with. Better yet, how can you limit yourself when you (the server) are working for tips (like a commission) and you see an opportunity to make a tip (commission) and you don't take it? How are you going make a better living by always limiting yourself?

It is so frustrating to see the missed opportunities and so worrisome to think that our business growth relies on people who don't <u>want</u> to grow. We won't grow if missed business opportunities are not limited or eliminated.

GETTING GUESTS BACK

How much it costs to get an upset guest back into your restaurant is astronomical in comparison to the amount it would have taken to greet and make that guest's experi-ence good to start with.

On Super Bowl Sunday, a few years back, with an MIT (manager-in-training) in tow, I appeared at the door step of a guest who had written in about a poor experience she had had a week or so earlier. I brought an apology, a basket of flowers, and a pass for a complimentary meal (for her and her guest) the next time she was in to dine with us. I left no strings attached other than I wished to have her feedback about her next visit.

Although the time investment in this situation should be clear, and that the cost was not insignificant, the time to follow-up should not be ignored, either. Do you think that we did too much, too little or the right amount in this situation?

The cost to satisfy this guest was much greater than the average spent to satisfy guests. The residual affect of bad and good experiences is something that cannot be measured accurately, but it is great. Something had to be done. It does not matter what you do as long as you do something.

The comparison of the greeting cost to recouping cost should never have to take place. As restaurant managers, our job is to make sure ***EVERY SINGLE GUEST EXPERIENCE*** is as good as it can be.

"People, help me out...!"

We, as managers, should not have to greet every individual guest as they are seated or as they enter; but, we should have instilled in our employees what it takes to give every single guest that first rate immediate greet and service.

Equipping our employees with the proper tools is our first priority. The last thing we want to do, and it so often does happen, is not plan for expansion, improvement, improving sales, etc. We also require the employees in our charge no room for error and all too often no room for creativity.

What happens when we as a company decide that we must change directions, it is a big stinkin' deal, rocks the boat and temporarily throws the balance out of kilter (whatever a "kilter" is... and why is it in a restaurant?)

Sometimes all individuals want is to show up for work and be told what to do, and then do it. Creating an environment to do this is challenging, and the target of a "perfect" environment should always be our focus; at the same time, room for "wag-ing it" (wild angle guessing) is necessary.

And, so the next step is setting all this up… which is what we all are trying to do… through schedules. Read on….

[Note: at the end of each chapter, there will be the "EGP" factor list revealed on what to take from that particular chapter to help you first **E**xist, then **G**row, and finally **P**rosper. These are the different levels I strive to achieve in my restaurant. At the end of this book listed are all 36 of the EGP Factors that will be a good list to refer to as quick reminders about each chapter.]

Chapter 1: Employees: EGP Factors:
1-Exist: You must have trained staff.
1-Grow: Raise your employees' abilities.
1-Prosper: Identify the future leaders quickly and exploit their talent.

CHAPTER 2
SCHEDULES
The Schedule is never done.

The ideal schedule does not exist nor is there ever a finished schedule. Scheduling many employees to do the various jobs is never easy and the schedule is in a constant state of flux. This is due to the fact that people's lives are in a constant state of flux. Understanding this first is a battle half won when it comes to figuring out the most efficient schedule to run at the volume you are planning on.

There's another rule, volume can hardly ever be exactly predicted. I think that most people would like to know exactly how their day is going to go but there are too many unpredictable things that cause their direction to be veered from its original path. Having a little bit of the "let's wing it" attitude is necessary to handle the various, unscheduled situations that we will encounter every shift we work. Having individuals working for you that expect everything to go exactly as planned is part of the business. Keeping the number of people working for you who create problems (worry that things go exactly as planned) to a minimum is necessary to make it through each shift.

Many people are in a bigger hurry than they know. This can be good and bad. We can schedule employees to handle volume that we know about but we must have them trained and equipped to handle fluctuations thereof.

The phrase "in the weeds" is often used in the restaurant business to mean you are in one of those situations when you do not have enough people to handle the volume you are experiencing. Other phrases used to describe peak volume are "covered up", "blown away", "swamped", etc.

There are as many phrases as there are eating establishments. I had not been in my first management position long when I wrote my interpretation of "peak volume" likening it to a "monster", of sorts, that we welcomed and tried to tame every time it visited. It was the slower volume time of the year so we had a skeleton crew on much of the time.

THE BUSINESS
"The Business is a funny thing,
One minute it looms over us,
Readying itself to pounce upon us ,
And, sometimes, as quickly as the next,
It's sleeping, lying still.
We often expect its roar,
Though seldom it's heard this time of year.
But when we least expect it, it is on us,
Clawing, scratching, screeching and clamoring:
It surrounds us, envelopes us in sound and movement.
When we're not ready for it, we turn to run
Only to be stopped short -
As if our shirt tails were stepped on.
We can handle it; it's only "The Business"
Nothing more, nothing less.
Oftentimes its countenance is unrecognizable -
We do not know it when we see it.
Once it's here, there's no mistaking it for anything else,
We can't fight it; we tolerate it and mostly enjoy it,
Indeed if not for what it is, then for whom it delights.
G. Steven Hearing, written in early 1985

Personifying - or, if you will, "monsterfying" - something inanimate like overwhelming business seems to give one the ability to dictate how it to handle it. We can only contain it and try to combat the carelessness or minimize the pitfalls of situations like these without unbalancing the labor to handle such things.

BALANCE

Labor "balance" is almost an impossibility. Think about it, if we had just the right amount for the business we were expecting, then that is all the business we could handle, theoretically. If we scheduled to do more business, we better do that business or we have thrown off the balance of profitability. But, we could not do the extra business without the extra labor; therefore, we did not have extra labor, we had just enough. It is as much gambling as it is to roll dice in a "crap game."

Reaping the results of "short labor" will be short lived. If we run short on labor, we will reap the benefits of more money on the bottom line because we spent less money to gain the sales; but, the inferior service we give to our clientele will cause them to go elsewhere thus causing our sales to go away.

Conversely, if we use too much labor, we are not maximizing our profitability because we have wasted some of our resources unnecessarily.

One of the most important areas of flexibility needs to be in the area of scheduling. There is a fine line that makes up the "point of diminishing return" here because of the fact that you do not want too much or too little labor to present the product to consumers.

POINT OF DIMINISHING RETURN

Often I have said that the characteristics of a good employee are the same as a bad employee. The good employees have the characteristics of sensitivity, strong will, salesmanship and empathy: a good balanced amount of each of these and you have a good employee.

Like so many other things, there is a point of diminishing return in these characteristics. If an employee has too much sensitivity, then he/she may give in too much to the person that wants something; too much strong will, and she/he will not give enough. If an employee has too much salesmanship, then it puts too much pressure on the patron; too much empathy, and we have lost the ability to make money by selling what we need to sell.

This theory works in other cost areas as well. If we have too many small wares, than they get lost, wasted, broken or otherwise put out of use; too few, and we rush to clean them and we lose them that way, creating a downward spiral below the equilibrium point - the point of diminishing return.

With food, we don't watch our usage and then we waste the extra and always try to skimp to get ahead to make up for the lost cost - thus compromising ourselves and falling below the equilibrium point.

"NONE TO TON" MENTALITY

Why is it when ever we run out of something that the next time we order it, we order twice as much as is needed? Also, when ordering a new shipment of product or supplies, trends are always in question, or should be, because the business plan is usually a very informed and therefore educated hypothesis - *or* guess! Always be wary of this.

GOOD EMPLOYEES SEE BIG PICTURE

When volume goes down, the best servers to go (leave your employ) are the ones that go first because they go after the money - that is why they are good. The ones who know how to make the most money are the ones who make you the most money.

At the point at which they leave and you are left with the inferior ones, then you have a "double-whammy" because the lesser ones will not make you as much money, and a downward spiral begins. Then the cycle broadens in concentric circles getting bigger and bigger like ripples on a lake. Eventually, you must do *something* – whatever it takes - to stop the spiral.

MAKING IT ON HIS/HER OWN

It is a beautiful thing when a server makes their first really great tip all on their own. The thrill of the tip is almost as much the reason why servers wait on tables, as money is the reason, because the thrill is great when it comes… yet often dejection is felt when a bad or no tip is left. This is the best motivator for a server than anything else can be. They earned it, yet they don't believe it when they get it.

LAST WAS BEST

It seems inevitable that employees will try to say that the last person doing the schedule was the best for two reasons:

1) People do not like change;

2) The last one to do it was familiar with availabilities and had a handle on strengths and weaknesses.

"WAY TO GO'S" GO AWAY TOO QUICKLY

Often we take for granted the things we do. But, the "sum of our experiences is our mettle" is what we must always remember. We do not always get to enjoy our successes as long as we would like, but we ourselves cannot forget them because we need to rely on what we have learned long before situations arise in order to know how to handle them.

I refer to these things in my mind as the experiences that I need to consult to solve future situations and I keep them in a mental "experience cupboard" to keep them handy when needed.

This leads to the next thing to address: the catchy, meaningful phrase, "situational management"… something we have learned to do with ever growing fancier names… but, the same thing nonetheless.

Chapter 2: Schedules: EGP Factors:

2-Exist: You must have staff.

2-Grow: You learn the capabilities of your best people.

2-Prosper: You exploit the capabilities of your best people.

CHAPTER 3
SITUATIONS
Situational Management

We have experienced the onslaught of computer training in the workplace and "virtual reality" CD-ROMs. Which, ironically, is an out of date phrase since now everything is "virtual-whatever". We are at the point of understanding and accepting that electronic programs are there for almost every situation. Next thing you know there will be_____ (fill in the blank and it will happen.)

Thomas Edison attempted to perfect the light bulb through trial and error. He made 10,000 experiments and still did not have it right and had faith that it could be done because he envisioned it. It finally became a reality.

No one really understands the pain and suffering that had to abound in his lab - and now we just flick a switch. It's not that we need to awe at the accomplishments of past successes all of the time. We can use these attempts of others to inspire and motivate ourselves to be and do just as great things.

In the power and splendor of the universe, inspiration waits for the millions to come. Man has only to strive for it. Poems greater than the 'Iliad', plays greater than 'Macbeth', stories more engaging than 'Don Quixote' await their seeker and finder.

-John Mansfield,
Poet laureate of England
('New York Times', June 1, 1958)

HANDS ON EXPERIENCE - These are the best teaching opportunities.

To me, the sum of all of my experiences is the teacher, the classroom for my knowledge that propels me forward.

We all could fill the air with past experiences that tell and enrich our lives and those around us. Many times as a manager, I have encountered situations where just the right words could help more than anything. Other times, no words would help, but just listening and not talking was the right thing.

Knowing what to do by recognizing situations is a valuable tool. I wish that I could tell you all of the things that you will encounter before you encounter them. Don't we all wish we knew what we were going to face just today, let alone over our careers. But my point is that we do nothing in vain, it all leads to our overall development.

So often I look to a certain point and think if I could only get *there* then there would be no more worries. Once I get *there* I see that there are more obstacles to overcome and "more miles to go."

This is our endeavor, to reach a never ending and always changing horizon. We have to have the energy and motivation to continue to the next point of regrouping, only to start again. To trudge forward to the next point of rest where we briefly stop to assess where we are and decide where we go from here.

We make these decisions everyday in life so we, all of us, are equipped to go on to the next point where we stop to decide where we are and where we are going from here. Our efforts are not fruitless, nor are they just an exercise in futility, but the substance of our experiences.

Mark Twain said that it is a "shame that we cannot start life at age eighty and work our way back to eighteen." Many people feel this way: so often we all are put in situations that we are not equipped to deal with and we know it. Knowing that we are not able to deal with it does not help and every situation cannot be simulated so as to learn from it.

You must "think on your feet" - a trite phrase used for years to signify that you are willing to try new things and get yourself into situations that are unfamiliar to you, but ones that you are willing to fight your way out of intellectually. Hearing about them helps a little more, but the best practice is being in that situation and working through it.

So often, in the past, I have looked to more experienced counterparts to help with advice. I feel that those who have been through a tough situation before would be better equipped with the experience to know how to resolve it.

Further, reading experiences in a book can only make you keener on knowing when you are in a situation with which you are not familiar.

READING VS. DOING

Reading about and experiencing situations that may possibly occur are very reasonable ways to gear up for whatever may happen to us at any time.

Situational management is almost always going to focus on extreme happenings. We hope that we all are equipped with the mettle to face the situations that occur each day. We must be ready for the rare events that seldom occur every day so we can be equipped with the know-how to face those circumstances.

Mock-ups of different situations will give us the experience of seeing how things might evolve into bad scenes. We then see how to face and resolve these situations by thinking through on our own or by watching others and then analyzing how we did.

Always expect something different or unusual to happen every day. In my career, I could say that every day something - even some little miniscule thing - happened to me for the first time.

KEEP PLUGGING (OR SLUGGING) AWAY

My motto was always to keep swinging. Whether I was in a slump or feeling badly or having trouble off the field, the only thing to do was keep swinging.

- Hank Aaron, (1934-) American Hall of Famer

So, we do not always know what we will face every new day but we are equipped with the knowledge of past experience to know to "keep swinging". With this "motto", we can face what is thrown at us everyday.

MENTAL INVESTMENT

The entire point of this treatise is that mental investment will pay off - but like with financial investment, it takes time.

For the initial investment to grow, time must go by and the growth occurs very slowly, but it grows.

Unfortunately, time cannot be sped up and the same results be yielded; thusly, more time yields more benefits.

A lot of trouble

The trees that are slow to grow bear the best fruit.

-MOLIERE

Often we have someone that is a lot of trouble to train and bring around into a more quality oriented skill arena. You have to ask if this person has the potential to do what is expected of him/her. At different points in their development, you may ask yourself if this individual is worth the time and effort that it is going to take to get him/her to an acceptable level of competency.

You may realize that the immediate cost in time and money may be harder to benefit from in the short run. Often the long term benefit is hard to determine immediately.

It is obvious that sending someone away early on may make it easier than keeping on with the training of standards, but sight of the long-term goal is important and ultimately the best way to go.

LONGEVITY: STAYING POWER

I have always thought that I could be a good "flash-in-the-pan" manager because I could see short term benefits very well, and could easily accomplish these things and in the short-term look like a hero. Maintenance of this great performance over a long period of time was always my goal and being a part of a team that achieved longtime results was always my desire.

Being part of a very enviable operation always brought comments like "I wish I was a manager at this store," and "it would be a dream to be a part of a smooth running store like this one."

These comments were the extra reward for working hard for many months to achieve the high level of success that elicited these comments. I always was quick to tell the ones who said these things about the operation I was part of, that there was work to do here.

Since that was the case, it would be reasonable to believe that the same level of success could be achieved anywhere with the right frame of mind and a commitment to never stop trying to achieve a great success level.

Breaking down the methods of achieving higher levels of success, by identifying how to traverse this path, would involve building on any and all success in increments. Once your level of success reaches a plateau, of sorts, you take what you are equipped with and use those characteristics to go to the next level.

If you find a path with no obstacles, it probably doesn't lead anywhere.

- FRANK A CLARK

Finally, situations have to be quickly deciphered to realize whether they are useful tidbits that will enrich our path to achieving our goals, or are they robbing us of our productivity. Reading on will elaborate and explain what I mean.

Chapter 3: Situations: EGP Factors:

3-Exist: Realize that things will not go exactly as planned.

3-Grow: Always work on contingency plans based on past experiences.

3-Prosper: From the very beginning of each shift "go with the punches" in order to avoid distractions.

CHAPTER 4
TIME ROBBERS
Plan to be Interrupted.

Many businesses, especially retail, have many distractions during the day. All distractions are opportunities for making or breaking one's job, business and career.

In this age of restaurant selections as diverse as anything can be, the next customer has to be convinced that he/she walked into the right place. It can easily turn into an experience that can turn-off potential return business.

Things that occur that can take your attention away from the customer cannot often be seen coming and before you know it, you are in the middle of something that is taking your eye off of your central focus.

These things can add up and make you have to do things over and over. I call these distractions "time robbers".

YOU ARE NOT ALONE IN MISTAKE-MAKING

Locking your keys in the office when you are the only manager on duty with keys at the time can be devastating. Knowing that it has happened to others can make you feel not as stupid - there is comradery among those who mess up!

I remember a time I locked the keys in the office in one of the places I worked. In this particular location, it was an old building with additions and old unused rooms in it.

I walked into the room next to the office that was used for minor miscellaneous storage; I attempted to see if I could access the office through the drop ceiling over the office. I lifted the tile in the storage room and reached over the partition wall, I was able to lift one tile of the drop ceiling over the office, and saw the keys, some six to eight feet away.

I wondered how to reach them, then I noticed on the top of the drop ceiling over the office there was a set of coat hangers bent together to make a rod about six to eight feet long with a hook on the end!!

Obviously this was not the first time this had happened and my predecessor left the tool needed for the job at the most convenient location! (Making some habit of keeping your keys from being lost or out of your possession is one of the most obvious things to keeping your focus clear … and your keys handy!)

Another time robber (TR) is the constant interruptions of legitimate things that must be discussed with employees (business or job performance, benefits oriented, etc.) that plague one throughout the day.

Having a time set aside to deal with miscellaneous details of one's job, or whatever concern it is, is a good way to be more productive. The result of the conversation that you have may not always be what your subordinates want, but this may yield some benefits none the less.

A particular applicant came into my operation one day during a busy time for me. She asked if we were hiring and in some way her understanding was that we were not hiring. The next day, she realized that I was somewhat distracted when she came in and she returned to ask again if there was any opening that she could apply for. Another manager talked to her and she was hired.

Letting the tasks of the day run me, instead of me taking charge of the tasks of the day, caused me to abandon my normal routine of interviewing applicants and it almost allowed me to lose a good employee before I knew her potential. She ended up staying with us for quite some time, moved into more positions and eventually moved into a management position.

Ironically, this same individual had another issue several years after that probably due to the reason of not giving undivided attention to detail due to "time robbers." She had transferred to another store where she had her paperwork botched up. She spent eighteen months there and transferred back to our store.

When she received her vacation check, I noticed that her recorded "years of service" was incorrect. I made a call to payroll and found out her transfer was not handled properly. The snafu was fixed and she received proper compensation.

Taking the time to do it right the first time would have saved more work later. *"If you don't have Time to Do It Right the First Time, When Are You Going to have Time to Do It Over."*(But, the fact that I "un-rehired" her, on paper record, made up for not hiring her on that day before we did hire her!)

Sometimes taking time like this makes the concern to be better understood and this is better for all involved and may help overall morale.

TIME TO INTERUPT

There are many things that can rob you of your time every day. The day you have planned for yourself may take unexpected turns, taking you in completely different directions from what you planned.

Planning on being interrupted sounds counter-productive, but if you plan on them, then they can be more productive.

THINK ON YOUR FEET

"Keep on going and the chances are that you will stumble on something, perhaps when you are least expecting it. I have never heard of anyone stumbling on something sitting down.

- Charles F. Kettering (1876-1958) American Inventor

Using the "thinking on your feet" theory, when things are thrown at you, you are equipped with the ability to turn the "time robbers" into opportunities to achieve something in a more efficient way.

Often things that are hurriedly done or accomplished in a slightly different way are not necessarily bad. New ways of doing things opens us up to seeing a variety in ways of achieving desired results.

Expecting the unexpected is part of the job. Being ready to do something in a different way should be the mindset you have. New and sometimes exciting ways to do things is borne out of the potential time robbers.

Read on to see more on the ideas of time robbers leading to better accomplishments….

Chapter 4: Time Robbers: EGP Factors:

4-Exist: Realize that things will happen to you to disrupt your schedule

4-Grow: Plan on interruptions and allow time for them in your schedule.

4-Prosper: Look at your planned day and anticipate what will be your distractions and try to eliminate them.

CHAPTER 5
ACHIEVEMENT
"Work For Food"

If you don't come into to work each day with a goal or thought of some type of achievement, then you have cheated yourself out of some development to be better, or your employer out of what he is paying you for.

Do you think that your employer just wants you to show up or think of ways of growing the company only on certain days? Of course not, the company wants every day to count for every employee, not just some days to count for some employees, or just some employees to make every day count.

The most important member of the company may seem to be the president or some high ranking company officer, but it is actually the person who is representing that company every day in the best way possible.

So often I have seen employees that show up not wanting to rock the boat or be bothered by having to do something that day.

I make a comment like "today you are going to have opportunities to help people that you haven't had the chance to help before in ways that will be fun and exciting" and they look at me like, "oh yea, you want me to do your job…" : they are reluctant to do more than they had planned to do that day.

It would be nice to show up and get paid for just being here, but we are here to earn our keep. The great orator and preacher John Wesley once was asked to come into the chamber with the deciding body of men in that church organization just after they had decided that he was to receive a raise.

When he was told how much of a raise he would receive out of the church budget, which was entirely amassed upon donations during worship services where he preached, he said, "oh no! Why did you do that? , it's hard enough to preach well enough to collect the money you are paying me now!"

No one is going to do our jobs for us; no one is going to collect the pay for us but ourselves. We must daily choose to take up the weapon we have chosen to wield, go out of our humble abode, accomplish something and come home for respite and sustenance to do it all again the next day.

Consider the Cheetah, he has to go out daily, in order to live, and hope that he can catch a gazelle. The gazelle has to daily go out and out run the Cheetah in order to survive another day.

UNLEASH INTENSITY

On the other hand, we must unleash the intensity that our employees have.

A horse in captivity longs for a carrot. If you dangle a carrot in front of a horse so long that he feels he will not get it, he then gives up the desire for that carrot, and just reaches down before him and eats the grass.

We must give our employees attainable goals and then let them enjoy the fruits of their efforts.

Several restaurant companies have gone south because the rewards were promised, not given as greatly as they were promised and then taken away altogether. What happens then is the best managers leave to go find more attainable carrots (rewards).

George S. Hearing

MOST IMPORTANT PERSON

The most important person that works for a retail company like a restaurant is the front line employee. To the next patron of your establishment, the front line employee who is helping the patron is the most important person for the company because he/she is the one that is going to give the service that patron expects.

If the experience is not good, then the company is not good in the eyes of the patron. It will be hard to retain the person's business or induce that patron to come back just based on that bad experience.

Conversely, a good experience is going to loom just as large in the eyes of patrons as indicative of the performance of the restaurant.

KNOWLEDGE ~ ABILITY

Knowing the notes of a song, being able to identify them, doesn't make the song sound good. Knowing words is not necessarily all it takes to write some worthwhile masterpiece. Skill to put together words is what makes a difference.

Another demonstration of making something great out of humble surroundings is exemplified in the poem "The Master's Hand".

The poem is about a skilled violin player who picks up an old, worthless looking instrument and plays it beautifully showing how well the violin can be played.

The components are not as great separately as they are as the whole.

The Hinkle family rocking chair endeavor is a great example. The component parts are less expensive (if you break one and happen to need a new piece) than the whole chair is: the craftsmanship is what you are buying.

This is true for so many things. "Conspicuous consumption", as The Great Gatsby put it, is what the draw is. Everyone wants the thing that someone else has. It is special to many therefore it must be a great thing.

The craze that made the Beanie Baby stuffed toy so popular has subsided. Is it because everyone has some of them or because the supply dropped? Who knows why fads come and go? If someone had that figured out, then he would be a tycoon.

"Branding" these days is very valuable: a name on a product is its intrinsic value nowadays, instead of just quality.

The McDonald brothers, Don and Maurice, started selling great hamburgers in a very profitable way. They were good at one part of business - efficient business methods.

They did not feel that their concept as it was would be marketable as McDonald's when they ventured out to sell their way of doing business as a franchise.

They then met Ray Croc and capitalized on his marketing skills. He developed the concept and sold many franchises of the business that the McDonald brothers started.

Today we have great knowledge of the efficient operation that is McDonald's.

The "brand name" that is associated with the product is what markets and sells the product. Eating out is often more of a choice of what "brand" of food and service is desired as much or more as type of cuisine and/or price.

This attitude of eating a certain brand has come to be a way of deciding on dining. A stigma of good service and bad service sometimes can influence people's decision of where to eat. Many decide on the brand of food based on past experience of that brand, thus subtle marketing is going on all of the time.

Our past achievements have been the things that influence future decisions for those of us who work in this business *and* the ones who patronize our business.

It is impossible to know what the next craze or fad will be. Like I said, if it was known, then someone would latch on to that idea and become wealthy cashing in on the craze.

Only one thing is certain: what is unknown is uncertain, using what you know is certain. Using your past achievements to try to succeed in the future is a

Mealfest

safe way to approach your work. You know that what you have succeeded at before has a high percentage to work for you again.

As you read on, you will see that a formula to follow will work just as it has worked to get you where you are now. We all need to realize that we have achieved success just by arriving at the point in time we are today.

To continue to succeed, we must use discipline, determination to develop what we have learned, and depend on that to keep succeeding.

Chapter 5: Achievement: EGP Factors:

5-Exist: Work to develop yourself and staff daily.

5-Grow: Realize that you and your staff can make a difference and achieve a higher level of greatness.

5-Prosper: Using your past achievements to succeed in the future is the way to approach your work.

CHAPTER 6
DEPENDABILITY, DISCIPLINE, AND DEVELOPMENT
Going in the right direction develops you and others

We have let systems and methods that work in some situations (like "best practices") prevail and attempt to make the whole company, that might have other successful components for instance, adopt a whole new way of doing things because it works in one application.

I contend that there are numerous right ways to accomplish goals and different ways should be allowed.

I have failed over and over in life. And that is why I succeed.

-Michael Jordan

The wrong way of doing things is the "teacher" that tells how to do things the right way. With knowledge of what does not work, we can go forward by avoiding that way of doing something again.

It seems that people (potential charges) always look to someone for guidance and direction. One way to get a daily dose of direction is to read something that can teach you something, anything, even if it is only fleeting and is all but totally forgotten once you begin the tasks of the day.

This is why e-mail is so popular and e-mail jokes and "hmm-isms" are often passed around. In the days before e-mail, one mind-starting thing to do was to complete the crossword puzzle.

I think that it should still be a mind-callisthenic to complete the crossword. When you read the crossword the clues are telling you to think in different ways. For example, a word that could be a noun or a verb is listed and you look at it and decide which best fits in the squares provided. Once you see how others fit around that set of squares you realize and verify whether you are right or wrong.

Now, this is not a mandate to stop working and start doing crossword puzzles(!), but getting into a routine that awakens your mind so you can be ready to open the minds of those around you is important.

DEPENDABILITY

Being a dependable individual is very important in this business. We rely on many people to work on a tight schedule; one that we have carefully planned and logistically fit together many factors.

If we are planning on having a truck full of food and wares show up at 6AM, then we plan on having several individuals there to unload it.

If we are planning on having a large group of people there at a certain time then we plan on having employees there to handle the group with the proper balance of cooks, servers and prepared food.

Obviously logistics are important. Armies who have been successful on the fields of battle have had very good logisticians setting up the scenario to have a victorious outcome long before the first engagement of the enemy takes place.

Similarly, we must operate from the point of view that the plan must be in place in order to succeed long before we attempt to serve the first meal and wait on the first table of patrons who walk in the door.

Also, we never have the weapon of propaganda: what you see is what you get.

When I hear about people making vast fortunes without doing any productive work or contributing anything to society, my reaction is, how do I get in on that?

-Dave Barry, in Miami Herald Humorist

We probably would all be lying if we said we totally loved our work and we would do what we do for the fun of it. We mainly show up to do what we do for a paycheck and other perks, but we would like to at least *like* our jobs.

On the other hand, it would be a great job if we were paid to achieve nothing; but it would not be very fulfilling. So feeling like we make a difference is a plus, and it is a good way to make a living.

DISCIPLINE

[Discipline is from the Latin root word "to learn". It also is the same root word that student comes from: example, *disciple*.]

We are taught that we must achieve our own way in the world, and we must direct ourselves to succeed. We are constantly learning things whether we see what we learn or not.

Disciplining ourselves is often harder than disciplining others. In our positions, when we show discipline of ourselves, we outwardly show what is expected of those we are in charge of managing.

Determine what goal you want to achieve. Then dedicate yourself to its attainment with unswerving singleness of purpose, the trenchant zeal of a crusader.

-Paul J. Meyer, American Author and Motivational Speaker

"A supervisor/manager/team leader needs to be self-motivated."

If this statement makes your shoulders slump, then hold on. You must re-think about what you are doing and where you are. You must decide if you are dreading the day *or* your career choice.

Granted, hardly any kindergartener would say to you that he/she wants to be a restaurant manager when grown: we just ended up here!

But the choice to do this is not a bad one just because you have to "jump-start" un-motivated employees… including yourself… each and every day… often the same ones… ones that do not want to make decisions for themselves… ones that will be washing dishes at age 70 when you will be enjoying the fruits of your years of saving in your 401k!

Make your work fun and you will be successful at it. Albert Schweitzer said "happiness does not equal success, but success is being happy with what you do." If you enjoy what you do, it will show and it will rain down success on you.

Dedication: this takes a lot of self-discipline

A leader takes people where they want to go. A great leader takes people where they don't necessarily want to go, but ought to be.

-Rosalyn Carter Wife of Jimmy Carter 41st President

DEVELOPMENT

My first job out of college was something I happened on in a strange way. I had stayed behind on my college campus after graduation due to the fact that I had procured a house (to be a "house-sitter" for a vacationing professor) and found a temporary job closing up a portion of the campus for the summer.

On the day I was to leave the campus, for the last time (because I had graduated), I ran into, quite by accident, the Director of Admissions. He struck me from the moment I arrived on the campus as a freshman, as being a gregarious and humorous man. Our conversations were always pleasant and animated.

He had selected me to be a "Trouble-shooter", as an undergrad, for the Office of Admissions. This was a prestigious position for a student to hold.

He nonchalantly asked me what my near future plans were. I told him of some plans that I had kicked around but had nothing definite planned. He told me of an Assistant Director of Admissions position that had just opened and asked if I was interested in interviewing

Mealfest

for it. I told him that I was and of my scheduled time of departure.

I had a hastily set-up interview later that morning, but I knew it wasn't good: all of my good clothes were packed and already shipped home - six hundred miles away!

You already figured out that I got the job. But the important thing to realize from this story is that the Director of Admissions knew that I "ought to be" in this position because he knew of the experience I had.

He was a great first boss to have and obviously had great experience in finding and developing new young talent in the endeavors of college admissions. He taught many of us that discipline of our abilities could yield great results.

I think that self-discipline is self-evident in the context of a work environment. Those who are getting ahead are the ones who discipline themselves to look past the mundane tasks we must accomplish daily.

Although these tasks are important, and we must make ourselves (and others) do them, their accomplishment is the pedestal that we must use to see where we want to go.

Now, even though this sounds a little metaphoric, let's see where it is going. In order to achieve more, one must have achieved the minimum requirements. Being true to yourself about your own job performance is paramount to succeeding.

Reality tells us that your biggest task, your biggest objective, should be not to get ahead of others but to use your own ability to increase your own performance.

- Zig Ziglar

Doing the best job you can, will be noticed - just like not performing well will be noticed - and it will swell you to new heights on evaluations, appraisals, assessments or whatever the latest buzzword is for performance reviews.

Often, we feel that as long as we can beat the people around us on performance reviews, then we are safe. It may also hold true that if you are out-performing some one around you in one area, they should be beating you in another area.

We should be competing with Indifference, Ineptitude, and Incompetence. We should not be competing with our team members, the ones who benefit along with us when we benefit; the ones who get to work with better developed staff; and the ones who get to go up in rank and income when the entire operation does succeed.

Great leaders don't create great followers, they create more great leaders.

-Tom Peters in <u>Fast Company</u>

Those around you are becoming great leaders if you let them and they let themselves. Competition can be a great thing if you view it and use it the right way.

Read on….

Chapter 6: Dependability, Discipline, and Development: EGP Factor list:

6-Exist: Surround yourself with dependable people.

6-Grow: Motivate your staff by showing them how you discipline yourself to complete tasks.

6-Prosper: Identify individuals who show potential and aid them in their development to be what they can be.

CHAPTER 7
COMPETITION
Who's breathing down your neck?

You'll never realize your full potential in business or athletics unless you're challenged. The breakfast of champions is not cereal, it's competition.

-Harvey Mackay, American Businessman and Motivational speaker

Competition is not a bad thing. Competition is a must in any society. In our capitalistic society it is what causes and encourages new and better, more efficient, thus profitable, ways of doing and accomplishing almost anything.

No one wants to have slack competition: me competing with you and you competing with me makes us both better. In the restaurant business, we are not only competing for "dining-out" dollars but also entertainment dollars.

The word "entertain" is from two Latin words: "inter" which means "between", and "tenere" which means "to hold". We are entertained by doing something that is a break from the "real" things in life. That which "holds us between" the times of reality in our lives is one of the things we need to rest and refresh ourselves: satisfying our spiritual hunger, as it were.

We often feel that we are guilty of some shameful pleasure when we entertain ourselves. Eating out seems to be a functional way to get a break from the fast paced reality of the world today (to be entertained) *and* to satisfy our physical hunger. (Remember "eat-a-tainment?") This makes the dining out experience important and it stands out more in the eyes of many.

FAMILY TIME

Many families have so little time together anymore that eating out is family time together that can be enhanced with good food and service.

Conversely, if the experience was not up to expectations, or if it was bad, you better hope the family fellowship was good for the patrons so as not to ruin the whole endeavor for you and for them.

We feed one table at a time, many times over and over. The goal is to please all the table-fuls of people. Quickly go to work on tables with bad experiences to try to salvage that particular one, analyze what went wrong to prevent the next bad experience, thus you learn something and make something profitable out of a mistake.

<u>Then, of course, are the guests who try to get something for nothing…</u>

"Everyone has a little larceny going on," Bing Crosby said in the movie *White Christmas* rather cynically. Fact is, many patrons come and go daily in many establishments, some with motives that are hard to determine.

If they are defrauding a restaurateur and trying to get free meals they are causing more havoc than they know.

This is of no concern to them. But they are complicating things to a great extent by making us plan against false business, thus hurting not only that day's sales, but clouding the trend that we create to encourage us to project sales and costs.

Communication is the key to avoiding any further damage to the business. You cannot over communicate situations in which someone is trying to harm your business.

George S. Hearing

WINNING: PUSHING THE WINNER

In high school, I graduated near the top of my class. I also excelled in track, garnering a scholarship offer to college. In academics whenever I or one of my highly ranked classmates couldn't "get" something, we helped each other out. Actually, on major projects that required partnerships, we would pair up to try harder to do better, thus raising the standard for excellence.

In athletics, for three years one particular teammate and I dominated the entire state in the high hurdles. This domination culminated in finishing the state meet in the top two spots in the high and low hurdles at the end of the third year and our team winning the state track meet.

We were talking after the event - the first state championship of any kind our 75 year old school had won to that point. I was ribbing him for one of the few victories I had had over him in our careers.

He turned serious on me and pointed out the fact that I being right on his heels for so long was what made him run harder and thus achieve more victories because he knew I would catch him if he let up any at all.

I in turn said that if he wasn't running so hard and making me chase him so hard, that I would not achieve the high finishes I always did.

We had mutual admiration, respect and empathy for the other's role in our own development.

Super-subs

In Tom Peters 1990 book "Liberation Management", the author expounded on the fact that some companies have contracted out some of the most vital, yet easily detached, business functions to companies that do a good job with that particular function. These so-called specialty companies were called, in his words, "super-subs."

He touted the fact that these "super-subs" were able to concentrate on the immediate problem without having to stop working on another project.

It makes sense then that a company would employ an expert to complete a vital *part* of the whole task, expertly, than to try to do that particular individual part with less expertise.

For instance, at one point in time, Cracker Barrel was trying to find a company, any company that made a better quality oil lamp to go on the tables in the dining areas.

It was so hard to find one that a company VP had to drag, "kicking and screaming"(in his words), an oil lamp manufacturer into a better quality product "arena"!

The company that made the lamps thought the lamps were good enough; but they could not withstand the wear and tear of the everyday use they were subjected to.

So once Cracker Barrel demanded a better quality product, and they were delivered one, they were a top purchaser of that product. They created their own "super-sub", and they got the necessary quality.

CHOICES ARE REAL

Many times throughout my career, and almost every single day my operation I am involved with opens up, I have said, "Will we receive any patrons today?"

I would always get incredulous looks from any body that was within earshot of my voice. (I think that this question is a holdover from ancient days when the bread winners of the family/clan/tribe went out to try to gain the sustenance to nourish the clan, tribe, or family group.)

It is something to truly think about and ask yourself each day you endeavor to continue your livelihood. I think that this is true of anyone who works at any level in any restaurant.

Fact is, choices are real and we should operate out of fear that we must be good enough today and each new day to get the business needed to survive.

All aspects of the operation need to point to this end. There are too many other restaurants out there to try and vie for our patrons everyday for us to think that people are going to come in just because we are here.

Stephen Jobs, the computer genius who co-founded Apple Computer, was and is a very charismatic leader of technical people. When his group was designing Apple's then new Macintosh computer, Jobs flew a pirate flag over his building. Its purpose? To signify his team's determination to blow the competition out of the water. (ref. H.Mackay, weekly article from Feb. 16, 2003)

Survival, moreover, the fear of not surviving, can be scary. One way to tame this fear is to decide ahead of time what helped you survive this day and copy that pattern of behavior the next time you vie for business.

There is an old saying in Africa that goes like this: "Every morning a gazelle gets up and knows that it must out-run the fastest lion or it will get eaten alive. And every morning, a lion gets up and knows that it must out-run the slowest gazelle or it will starve to death. So, whether you are a gazelle or a lion, every morning when you get up, you better be running."

Light tomorrow with today!

-Elizabeth Barrett Browning

Consistency can be difficult. Duplicating yesterday's performance can be daunt-ing in so many ways. But, you must achieve the minimum setting you had before in order to build more.

Just as a chapter ends and a new one begins, so do your business days: consistently....

Chapter 7: Competition: EGP Factor List:

7-Exist: Competition is a must in every society.

7-Grow: Your competition makes you better.

7-Prosper: Compete with yourself to consistently beat your previous best performance.

CHAPTER 8
CONSISTENCY
Do your job the same way, the right way, everyday.

Integrity - always (times) and in all ways (directions) - must be maintained by the manager and should be by others.

Money often is the cause to cross the line of integrity, and no amount of money can effect the restoration of integrity. At the risk of venturing too far on the morality issue of business, it is never right to do the wrong thing, nor is it ever wrong to do the right thing.

Making money is the goal of our business - after all, would we show up to work if we did not get paid? - but not at the expense of integrity of our employees or ourselves.

This is good business sense even if at the end of that day we don't seem to have grown the business as much as we had a goal to do. In other words, do not let greed or <u>desperation</u> rule your attitude or performance when it costs you integrity on anyone's part.

Too Big for Britches

"Whatever you want in life, other people are going to want it too. Believe in yourself enough to accept the idea that you have an equal right to it."

- Diane Sawayer (1945- American broadcast journalist

Companies in the past have decided that they know the direction a company needs to go and they know all of the trends well enough to know that just about anything they do will be successful.

In the 1990's, Cracker Barrel tried a new concept. The "Corner Market" was born and with much fanfare it was touted as the next new craze in meals away from home. It was going to supply meals to go for families on the go. The trend never caught on completely and it was closed after a few unsuccessful years. The new concept did not ever approach the success of the main concept.

On a smaller scale, some managers think that a store that is doing well always has done well, that is the place to go. They naively think that the store just automatically always did and will always do well just because it has... like no effort was put into making that store a great store and the management team has always enjoyed the smooth operation and nothing was done by them to achieve the high level of consistency and success.

To lift a store (or a company) up to pedestal status is not good, at best, and can be devastating, at worst. One good thing about going through bad times is you remember the negative well enough to not repeat them. If one has not had the experience of a bad situation, then when and how does one learn how to handle a crisis never faced. So in order to know how good the good times can be, you must first know how bad the bad times can be.

Furthermore, companies must be wary and respond to changes. Rolling with the punches makes one a better, stronger, fighter and able to respond to rapid changes. Things that were always done the same way may have to be done differently or left out altogether.

Consistency in this case would be limited to what works - not just doing something over and over again for consistency's sake.

SUPERVISORS' BEHAVIOR (cynical view)

Executives of companies are always checking to see if you are doing your job. Two reasons why they do this:

1) Because they were always trying to do things the easy/lazy way and they know you are, too;

2) Their supervisors did it so they do too.

One way to get the big wigs to be happy/stay away is to do your job the same way, the right way, everyday.

CHANGE

"It is not because things are difficult that we do not dare; it is because we do not dare that they are difficult."

- Seneca (4? B.C.-A.D.65) Roman philosopher, dramatist, and Statesman

We are faced with challenges every day that we must decide whether or not to go around, through or over. In other words, we must first see the challenges and identify that they are challenges and opportunities to make us better by going through them. Once identified, then the time for action is there. The first solution that you come up with may not always be the right one. I am reminded of the Lilliputians who tied up Gulliver upon first discovery of him only to have him quickly break loose after their great efforts to achieve

Mealfest

such a big task… yet they pressed on and came up with another solution.

Not making a decision is making a decision to not do something. We all make decisions everyday and they are not always good ones. So when we decide to do nothing, leaving a problem or dilemma unsolved, then we are not doing our jobs. In other words, making decisions - good or bad - has to be our job and the fear of making a wrong one must not stop us from making one. The only wrong decision is not making one.

Worry does not empty today of its sorrow, it empties today of its strength.

-Corrie Ten Boom Dutch evangelist

We can worry and do nothing, or we can make decisions and stick by them even when we learn it was wrong: for wrong decisions teach us too. Like I said, the only bad decision is the one not made. Every day we do things and say things and they seem insignificant. What we do is always under a microscope and we are setting standards by our conduct and manner of managing every day.

A single day is enough to make us a little larger, or, another time, a little smaller.

- Paul Klee (1879-1940) Swiss expressionist painter

We are influencing those "in our charge" all of the time whether we mean to or not. Standards are changing by the very method by which we do anything.

Remaining consistent in this since is hard by the fact that we must realize that the standards are to be adhered to all of the time. Conversely, by following standards consistently, we know what is expected of us and our employees know what is expected of them. In a sense, we create a "bank" of solutions to common problems.

This is ultimately the best way to operate. We often have employees in situations where they want to say, "What am I to do in this situation?" and they should know the answer by consistently seeing the way it was handled before.

Therefore, the solution to a problem is simple and understood by all. Having a bank of problem solving answers should be the norm in any operation.

Furthermore, the right answer does not always stay the right answer, so revisiting this "bank" should be a regular routine. When the answer changes, "withdraw" the old "right" answer and "deposit" the new "right" answer. Then this must be communicated to all who rely on this "bank" of answers.

Surrounding yourself with a good core group of employees should always be your internal mission. One cannot immediately identify "good" employees. Some may be inspired by you or your organization to higher capabilities.

Always watching for emerging great skills or qualities is our task as managers. Beginning with recognizable skills is always helpful. We see many who want to work for us, or at least they say they do.

An open ear as well as discernability in what people are telling you should always be our stance. Read on to gain a little more insight on interviewing prospective new employees.

Chapter 8: Consistency: EGP Factors:

8-Exist: Do your job the right way, everyday.

8-Grow: Realize that you are being watched and emulated at all times.

8-Prosper: Watch for emerging consistent skills in your staff to see future leaders.

CHAPTER 9
INTERVIEWING

In this business of rampant turnover, managers have the opportunity to interview many applicants. I have interviewed literally thousands of people. There is a huge amount of turnover in this industry, yet there does not have to be; less turnover can start with better scrutiny of the words you use and the ones you hear.

Some applicants actually tell you how undependable they are by telling you in interviews why they quit, how they worked and how they wanted (or did not want to) to work, and why they came to *you* to be the solution to all of these things. This is why there should always be a personal interview done on any and every individual.

We, our restaurant's tasks, are almost exactly the same; only the tasks have different names. "Culinary implement reclamation technicians" are still dishwashers.

Human nature is such that people are going to *do what you do* and probably not just what they tell you they are going to do. Nor will they always do what you *tell them to do*. The phrase "work with them and they will work for you" is true. If we as managers get in the groove and do some of the tasks that the employees in our charge are doing, then the results achieved are better, if not phenomenal. Coming together and achieving something as a group is also very fulfilling for all involved.

Camaraderie is not as prevalent as it used to be. "Old school managers", as I have often heard managers that are hard to work for referred to, still had camaraderie with those individuals who worked hard for them. It is hard to accurately pinpoint those characteristics in a short interview. Of course, if you asked them point blank about their camaraderie, the applicant is going to give you what he/she thinks is the most sensible answer. Looking for the subtleties of mannerisms, words used, attention to appearance, etc., are important factors in a personal interview.

Often I have hired folks that strike me as someone I would rather have working for me than with the competition. "We are always looking for good people…" is the pat answer I give when I am asked if we are hiring.

The acid test for hiring. *Ask yourself, "How would I feel having this same person working for my competitor rather than for me?"*

- Harvey Mackay, Businessman and Motivational Speaker

In an interview with a potential employee one should of course ask the obvious questions but always look for the not so obvious answers when the applicant is responding.

One manager I worked with said that he looks at the teeth of the person he is interviewing. He said that if the person's teeth seemed to be in good shape and cared for, then the person should be meticulous and prone to care about details - even small ones. Also, a person taking care of his/her teeth takes you to a level of confidence that this person is able, willing, and presentable enough to talk to your potential patrons. By contrast, when someone doesn't like their own teeth, they tend to try to hide their mouth when talking to someone and this leads to an air of discomfort. He thought this out (!) and then he made it his consistent measuring stick.

Another manager I encountered said a psychological trait that people tend to do is look up when they do not know an answer and they tend to look down when they are lying. We all have things that we sub-consciously and consciously do or follow. Body language sometimes tells you more than the words people are using.

REQUIRED AND REQUIREMENTS

In the past, I have encountered individuals that will tell you they are there for the sole purpose of satisfying an unemployment officer's compliance report. I have also encountered those who have asked what the pay would be and have told me that the public assistance program they are on pays them more than I am offering them to work for me. Sheer economics, I guess. Of course, you must ask, are they going to be a "go-getter" enough of the time to make a difference in your work force and therefore, are they worth going through the effort of hiring and training.

I have also seen an applicant write down their availability so restricted that the individual cannot possibly be scheduled in the situation they are asking for. Sometimes when they do this they are telling you that they don't really want the job.

Then there are the individuals who have a change in their availability as soon as you bring them on board. Be careful in hiring restricted scheduled applicants because they are the first ones, often, who cannot work when you need them.

Conversely, one of the best ways to fill out your schedules with individuals who can fill in during odd times is to hire those with very restricted requirements of work times. You just have to hire more employees. Sometimes identifying certain shifts that need to be covered can be enticing to the right applicants; and vice versa.

The whole point here is that there is no set formula to identify the "right" applicant all of the time. Sometimes availability is all it takes, sometimes just a "gut" feeling from what you have seen and heard in talking to this person. The most important thing to remember is that you should never feel like you do not need to be looking for more employees or an upgrade from the level you are on currently. The inevitable "warm body hiring" is something that all mangers have been guilty of at one time or another. This is never the right solution, but it can be overcome, one way or another.

THIS IS THE JOB OF A LIFETIME

Interviewing thoroughly will raise the value of the job in the eyes of the interviewee. Raising the worth of the job you are interviewing for, and how an applicant reacts to that, give you more helpful assessment information.

Demographically speaking, there are fewer and fewer people to interview and select from every year. Analysts conclude that by the year 2015, there will possibly be a shortage of as great as 40 million workers. ("Analyst forecast worker shortage", Gannett News Service, article by Chuck Raasch on 3/23/2003).

All of the interviewing, psychological testing, and interpretation of physical mannerisms can still go wrong: you don't know what the performance level of an individual will be until you have that person in the desired position and he/she is trained.

APPEARANCE

Appearance of individuals can be a telling factor also. Self-expression seems to be one of the most important things people are thinking about these days. Body piercing, tattoos, etc., seem to know no bounds anymore. How a company that treats its employees in regards to self expression is touchy, on one end of the spectrum, and raises concerns about personal hygiene on another.

The prejudice of the public is not something to be regulated by a manager; nor can one legislate self expression. But an appearance "code" can and must be administered.

GOOD EMPLOYEES

Are "good" employees really good or are they just the ones with the loudest complaints (the "squeakiest wheel" syndrome) and the ones who point out the most what they have done for you and the company? Sometimes we have someone who does an exemplary job - i.e., jumped in when needed in an unfamiliar position, came in and worked an unscheduled shift, eased the burden of someone in a particular situation, etc. - and then they won't let it be forgotten.

SUPERSTAR WANNABES - "CLARK KENTS"

I would contend that someone, who on a regular basis touts their own efforts over those of others, is really not a team player, but a "superstar wannabe". This person wants it to be known by all within earshot what exactly he/she did to help accomplish the feat achieved. The credit and recognition should always go to all involved. The superstar wants something extra and feels they deserve it. This is dangerous ground and this behavior should be held in check but in the most positive manner possible. Group recognition and encouragement is always good, but a sales contest, or some other measurement contest is always a good way to channel the competitive spirit of individuals.

The real team players, in my opinion, are the ones who quietly help where and when needed and shun notoriety and reward (the "Clark Kent's" of the world). Whenever you are having contests, these are the individuals who love the quiet recognition for their efforts they plug away at. They are the ones who feel they get rewarded weekly with a paycheck.

They are the ones who often do not get the best stations, but you want to give it to them. They are the ones who come in whenever needed, but you hate to bother them. They are the ones who when you ask them to do something to help the company, or the unit, they do not first ask "what's in it for me?" And you *want* them to tell you what they want for helping you, but they don't; and they never ask for something in return.

WE HAVE A LOT TO OFFER

Like I said earlier, in this new century we are seeing lots of people who felt like a good company future with good benefits and stability was an entitlement. Now many are feeling like everything they have in a job could slip away in a hurry with the next corporate audit.

They are seeing top managers of companies who took it all for themselves and left nothing for the bulk of the employees - the ones who made the company great for the top managers of the company.

Integrity is something that stands the test of time. It has to be engaged everyday all of the time. This is no easy task, but it is our job and it is what we are paid to do. The benefits and rewards are regular paychecks. Regular paychecks are a lot to be thankful for - just ask any employee of the failed and failing companies out there.

"IT'S OKAY"

Some of the executives out there were feeling like, "If I can get away with it, then it is OK." Where did this mentality come from? It seems that unchecked activity and hopes of accuracy were left to the wiles of company officials. They were given Carte-Blanche to do as they pleased because returns were so great. Personal accountability was non-existent in many of those in charge. Follow-up on those who could "cook the books" was not done or not done well enough.

ALL'S WELL

The overall economy enjoyed such unprecedented growth that all must have been well in every company. Indeed, internal pressure was that all needed to be well and growth needed to be the primary yield. Now we are prone to wonder how real all of the economic growth really was. Without integrity in the ranks of some of the CEO's, how certain are we that all of the growth was real?

HARD WORK

I have studied the lives of great men and famous women and I found that the men and women who got to the top were those who did the jobs they had in hand with everything they had of energy, enthusiasm, and hard work.

-Harry S. Truman

Many people since the early 1980's, when the economic times started getting better, have not had the hardship of looking for a job. Nor have they seen many bad investments. Or, worst of all, they are experiencing the fall of their companies without providing severance, retirement, or other benefits to those let go.

Jobs were appreciated more before. I know they will be appreciated more in the future. Before us is a future that may find them holding on to what they have and not job hopping, thus enriching their own lives and their career opportunities.

END AS BEGINNING

As the end of an interview is really only the beginning of employment, so is the performance of individuals who strive to do anything. The last part of this book (the last three chapters) is an explanation of how we do not ever arrive at the level of perfection that we all strive to achieve. The goal to be perfect is ever elusive, yet longed for at the exclusion of all others. True, this is frustrating, but it will be clear that we do not ever want to arrive at that point.

Our business in life is not to get ahead of others, but to get ahead of ourselves, to break our own records, to outstrip our yesterday by our today.

-*Stuart B. Johnson*

So, now you begin the end of this book knowing that you are ending with a beginning….

Chapter 9: Interviewing: EGP Factor list:
9-Exist: Do not do "warm body hiring".
9-Grow: Be consistent in questioning and standards.
9-Prosper: Ask yourself, "would I want this person working for my competition?"

CHAPTER 10
MUSINGS

"Going to a restaurant is ninety percent trust/ attitude and ten percent appetite."

This statement seems to be true because a person or group of people who are eating out want to go somewhere to functionally eat but aesthetically enjoy the surroundings, service, and quality of the cuisine they have chosen to eat.

Since we have become a society that loves dual functions - like eating out and getting entertainment - "eat-a-tainment" - we base future decisions on past experiences: a good experience eating out is as often remembered as well as bad experiences.

Furthermore, expectations not being met can cause an otherwise good experience to be less than it was the last time if the consistency is not there each visit.

To a point, having the same thing on a menu sometimes can cause people to return to get the same thing over and over again because they know they can count on it being good based on the last time they had that item.

Our own dilemma is that we hate change and love it at the same time; what we really want is for things to remain the same but get better.

-Sidney J. Harris, American author

But diners' desires or penchants for variety are obvious, too. The diversity of different cuisines out there at restaurants proves this point. Finding the right balance of current menu items to keep offering and mixing in new items to spark interest in new things is tricky but very important.

Understanding that people like what they have gotten before can save you in time and money. I once jokingly told a guest that since we no longer carried the item that he enjoyed the last time he was in, he would have to order off of the menu he had before him. He got so upset he left without eating. I found out a day or so later that he had told others what I had said and I sent an apology to him and an offer to buy him and three friends their meal the next time they were in. He took advantage of my offer to the point that it almost hurt. I learned a valuable lesson about loyalty to likes and dislikes.

Often people will not try new things because they know how faithfully good the item they want to order was each time they have ordered it in the past. So, ads only give us brand exposure; the attitude that the diner has about us is what makes them come back over and over again.

POINT OF DIMINISHING RETURN

Often I have felt that the characteristics of a good employee are the same as a bad employee; it is the different levels of these characteristics that make up each. The good employees have the characteristics of sensitivity, strong will, salesmanship and empathy: a good balanced amount of each of these and you have a good employee.

Like so many other things, there is a point of diminishing return in these characteristics. If an employee has too much sensitivity, then he/she may give in too much to the person that wants something; too much strong will, and she/he will not give enough.

If an employee has too much salesmanship, then it puts too much pressure on the patron; too much empathy, and we have lost the ability to make money by selling what we need to sell.

NONE TO TON MANAGEMENT

If we have too many small wares, then they get lost, wasted, broken or otherwise put out of use; too few, and we rush too much to clean them and we carelessly lose them that way, creating a downward spiral below the equilibrium point - the point of diminishing return.

With food, we don't watch our usage and then we waste the extra and always try to skimp to get ahead to make up for the lost cost - thus compromising ourselves and falling below the equilibrium point. Why is it when ever we run out of something that the next time we order it, we order twice as much as is needed? Also, when ordering a new shipment of product or supplies, trends are always in question, or should be, because the business plan is usually a very informed and therefore educated hypothesis - guess!

GIVE WHAT YOU ASK PAYMENT FOR

Seating patrons faster than the ability of the crew you have on duty is a way to "steal" the money of your patrons. It would be better to turn away potential patrons at the front door than to bring them in and serve them poorly then make them pay for something they did not get: good service.

The product that we are presenting must be worth what we are asking people to pay. If any attempt to give less than what's worth paying for is made, then we are robbing those who we try to collect from. It is our responsibility to provide the utmost quality for the price we ask.

GOOD EMPLOYEES GO AFTER THE MONEY

When volume goes down, the best servers to go are the ones that go first because they go after the money - that is why they are good. At the point at which they leave and you are left with the inferior ones, then you have a "double-whammy" (from the old game show where the "whammy" pops up to take away all of your money): because the lesser ones will not make you as much money, and a downward spiral begins. With the loss of revenue, the cycle broadens in concentric circles. The loss of good employees means less volume and then you have to cut cook's and other employees' hours to save labor, etc. The hardship eventually envelops the whole business.

Starting over with new servers, the sales force of your brand and product can be slow and tedious but is so necessary to develop and enrich that strong core of people that are "in-tune" with what's going on and want to make the business succeed.

The thrill is great when it comes… yet often dejection is felt when a bad or no tip is left. This is better motivation for a server than anything else can be. They earned it, yet they don't believe it when they get it. Conversely, when they get a bad tip (or none at all) then he/she must examine the type of service given and learn how to avoid that situation, if possible, in the future.

Often we all react this way: we work toward a goal then we are surprised when we actually *achieve* that goal. Once, I received a bonus of about 3-4 times bigger than I had ever received before. I made a point to thank my supervisor the next time he was in and he rather stand-offishly replied that I should not thank him because I had earned it. Also, I have taken responsibility when things were not running perfectly. When this happens, all you want to do is get back on track as quickly as you can in as short a time as you can. It is the same thing as the server mentality only on a larger scale.

A taste of the sweeter fruit of more money is definitely great incentive to get out there and do it over and over again. After all, we are in a business of relentless repetition and this can get mundane for us and cause us to lose our focus or competitive edge.

The mundane nature of the business appeals to some. There are workers who thrive on relentless repetition and are happy striving to do the same thing over and over, better and better, with fervor and excitement. The process of finding these folks can be daunting and expensive… but how can we afford not to find these folks and insert them into our operations?

So often we as managers think we can just "throw labor" at situations without regard to one's ability or his potential to achieve. It is of the greatest importance to find individuals to do what we do, along side, growing (rowing) as hard as possible to keep the shift (ship)

Mealfest

afloat and keep going forward, throwing aside the waste (waves) as we sell (sail) to new heights (horizons).

Okay, the analogy is not really an allegory… but it could be and the participants are you and your staff. I don't know about you, but I want my staff to be ready to achieve greatness, growing or rowing, selling or sailing, or otherwise.

I think that qualities of individuals can be recognized and developed to greater levels when necessary. All you have to do is investigate or interview as thoroughly as possible and then be ready to cut your losses if you were wrong about the person you hired to do what you wanted them to do.

Making these accomplishments become desired achievements in your staff can be taxing. Not making them can be devastating and expensive. If you do not have a good core crew to build on, then you will never be able to go anywhere near your goal of succeeding.

Winners surround themselves with other winners.

-Harvey Mackay

A good team is what it takes to achieve more than you can possibly imagine. This is the primary ingredient in the formula for achievement coming up next.

Chapter 10: Musings: EGP Factors:
10-Exist: See what others have to offer.
10-Grow: Learn from others.

10-Prosper: Realize that you are achieving great things and that others learn from you.

CHAPTER 11
FORMULA FOR ACHIEVEMENT
RISE to the next level.

EXPERIENCES

Many of us can think of good and bad experiences in places we have gone to eat. The first time in an eating establishment gives us that first impression that makes us not hesitate to come back or be leery of a return visit. Word of mouth is important in many ways. Diners always talk about where they went to eat.

I can remember a lot about dining experiences in the past. Most of all of the gatherings of good friends and acquaintances I can remember are surrounded by a time of getting together to eat. This is true for most experiences for most people.

The purpose of this book is to put a name to some of the tasks to be completed and goals to be accomplished.

RESPITE

The need to slow down in our fast paced society has never been greater. We need a brief respite from the hustle and bustle of the world. All of the experiences that one has should be examined and it should be determined what should be learned from these things.

INFORMATION

I like to share experiences with folks because it is the stories in one's life that teach us about things. I listen to older folks because they have probably read more books and had more personal experiences to tell stories about than what you can read in a book or look up on the internet.

Listen when individuals tell you something about their past experiences, it enriches your own experience by hearing it and making you more equipped to recognize that situation if the need ever arises, therefore it makes you better prepared to more quickly resolve it.

SUBSTITUTE

So often when I have gone to other stores to help out, all I have to do is go through the motions of what the physical task is.

Being a "rent-a-manager" is no where near as hard as doing the task of the day-to-day manager that you are temporarily replacing. He or she is the one that is charged with growing the staff, developing long range business plans, and knows the clientele that regularly frequents the establishment, among other things.

All I had to do was maintain and enrich that shift I was working. That was hard enough. Being in a strange place, with no one knowing your ability, and being called on to step right-in to unfamiliar surroundings, *and* make a difference… that was nearly impossible. Being able to do this is made possible by substituting your present surroundings with the one you are accustomed to and then you make the decision.

Being malleable and able to step right into situations makes you more valuable to the operation and it shows your willingness to grow to the level that is necessary to achieve more and raise your worth.

EMPATHY

We always admire the other fellow more after we have tried to do his job.

-William Feather

We cannot imagine the stress and mental strain it is to do what someone else is having to do. We can see the physical pace that one is going, but we do not know the mental activities of that person.

We may see some concern on the face of the one going through the activity of his job, and view his body language, but until we feel his same experience, we cannot completely have empathy for him and his task at hand.

TO...

THE NEXT LEVEL

If you followed the first letter of the headings above, then the acronym you spelled is the main formula for success:

<u>RISE TO THE NEXT LEVEL.</u> Our experiences in the past are what enable us to achieve this.

It should be obvious that you need to <u>RISE</u> to the next level in order to succeed. Before you can rise to that next level in your superiors' eyes, you must do it in your own eyes.

Visualizing yourself in that position is the best training you can give yourself to know how to take that position and succeed with it. Go one step further and work at that "next level".

What does it mean to go to that elusive next level? Is there a proverbial "next level" and why should we be wanting to get there? We will never reach the highest level so there will always be "the next level." We do not know what it is called, and we are not always clear on why we want to go to it. But, somehow we know it is where we want to be.

Our growth and achievement desires are what make us want to go there. What if we haven't achieved all we wanted to on this level? And if we go to the next level is it sacrificed? Or automatically achieved because we are on the next level?

Of course, this is just a catchy phrase, used to motivate individuals. The fact is, in the next chapter this will be addressed: that we should always want to be better. This is a seemingly hokey concept but one that all business growth is based on and should be based on.

THE RIGHT THING

We should all strive to do the right thing, which should be obvious, because we cannot survive in a state of suspicion. Temptation to be better has overcome many a trusted company officer. Going to the next level is of great concern and should be the goal of much of your activity. The wrong way to go to the next level is much easier, it seems, but the consequences are not worth the effort to rise with dishonesty.

Look at all of the lack of integrity in business in this young century: it has "come home to roost", as it were, and companies have fallen and the economy stumbles slightly with them.

It has not recently been as stable as it has in the past, but it will recover and we will continue to grow as an economy as we have before.

BE EVER VIGILANT

The level we are on is not the one to stay on, nor are our competitors staying on it. It is always changing. We must all watch so as to not miss the trip to the next level.

The last chapter is next, but only in this book… there will be no last chapter on achieving success.

<u>Chapter 11: Formula for Achievement: EGP Factors:</u>

11-Exist: Use what you have experienced to guide you.

11-Grow: Always glean experiences from others.

11-Prosper: Never stop rising to the next level.

CHAPTER 12
THE LAST CHAPTER: SATISFACTION

BEING THE BEST

Our own dilemma is that we hate change and love it at the same time; what we really want is for things to remain the same but get better.

-Sidney J. Harris, American Author

FINE IS GOOD, BETTER IS BETTER, BEST IS UNBEATABLE... until it's the standard then the cycle begins again...

The last chapter can never be written. Just as time goes on presumptuously into the future - knowing not what direction to go except forward - our careers will run their course as part of the flowing effluvium of time.

You cannot step twice into the same stream. For as you are stepping in, other and yet other waters flow on

-Heraclites (c.460B.C.)
Greek philosopher

We entered in and we extract ourselves out of this service industry just as a raft lets in and out of a river.

The careers that we have had are not in vain. Anyone in this business should congratulate himself/herself for being a part of raising the standard to where it is.

We strive to be better all of the time to try to reach the ever elusive goal to be perfect. Efforts feel as though they are in vain in that pursuit but we also realize that being perfect is an impossible goal.

Thomas Payne wrote the story of a fictitious place called Utopia. It was a place of perfection and it was a place to envy. There is no Utopia - so there is no perfect restaurant.

If there was a Utopia, by concept, we would not reap its benefits because a change in the balance of perfection tatters its perfection. For instance, say there was a place of perfection. This "Utopian community" would be perfect and then someone would come into the picture and have input to change something to make it better (criticize something).

Immediately the perfection is gone because someone knocks it. Knocking or criticizing things the way they are is the way to change them and make them better. Then when it returns to perfection again, the process will be restarted.

Critics point out our shortcomings and faults. Sometimes we're unaware of them; the critic helps us identify them.

Zig Ziglar

CHANGE IS INEVETABLE

If you surrender completely to the moments as they pass, you live more richly those moments.

-Anne Morrow Lindbergh (1906-2001) American writer

Everything is in a state of flux. The next product or service market trend is on the horizon, waiting to be seen. Once it is found, then there will be the inevitable improvements on it and then the new, better thing is perfected even more precisely because there are those who look at the new product or service and say, "this could be better…"; and once it has been improved, then the cycle begins again.

BETTER ALL OF THE TIME

The toughest thing about success is that you've got to keep on being a success.

-Irving Berlin

Whenever any of us does not say that something could be better, then we have "given up" or "given out". When a person asks you how business is, you can say "it has never been better" and in the same breath say, "but we can always do (be, have, et cetera) better" (or more).

The good business that you have now has to maintain that level of good you are now. Since "good" is a matter of opinion and perception, then staying there is difficult, especially in this "ever growing more fickle" society.

I do not believe you can do today's job with yesterday's methods and be in business tomorrow.

-Nelson Jackson, business leader

Top quality will always be topped. The best services will always be bettered. Food quality will always be refined to the best state possible. This industry should see no end to its boon because there will always be those coming along who take it a step higher, a level above the rest.

In competition, we always try to be better than the best guy.

The standard of measure is constantly changing because the next company to be "king of the hill" will soon be the last winner. We must top ourselves everyday.

"GREAT SERVICE"

Do not seek to follow the footsteps of the men of old. Seek what they sought.

-Basho (1644-1694), Japanese poet

The next level of competition we have will be our "great service". Even if we beat ourselves next year, we need to be different to do that. Whenever we raise our STANDARD of service, we must realize that the level of service we just gave had better be exceeded the next time.

This goes on beyond measure and the challenge to all of us is to be better all of the time. In other words, the "Best" has to be "Better" more often than being the "Best" in order to achieve the next level.

I have had to pick myself up and get on with it, do it all over again, only even better this time.

- Sam Walton (1918-1992)
American Businessman

It may sound like semantics, but the thing we all have to do is be "better" than the "best" we have done before, all of the time. It does not have to be a great or marked improvement: just a little better than before will do.

SUCCESS

Success is more a state of mind than it is a set of actions. If you are happy where you are, then you have achieved success.

-Albert Schweitzer

If one works at something and gets better at it and delivers the same high quality product or service every time, then he or she is successful.

Being better, un-noticeably, is a sign of success; but, the set of actions to achieve that success is ever changing just to keep the quality the same in the eyes of the receiver of the goods and services.

There is one thing that I have often remembered as being ironic. When I was in college, I had the opportunity to work in the school cafeteria as a choice of one of the work study jobs. The college offered an extra incentive to work in the dining hall: you would be given an extra thousand dollars in grant money to work there.

The irony was in the fact that a food service job in college was worth more money to the college than a position in another area. (Not to mention the fact that restaurant management was not an offering at the liberal arts college.) Of all the jobs I ever had, I enjoyed working in the food service business almost the most (I have to admit that I enjoyed all of my writing gigs, too).

The intrinsic value of what we do is not fully appreciated …except by those of us who strive relentlessly to make it happen everyday with our fellow heroes of the culinary front!

In final conclusion, since there is no end to levels of achievement, there will be much more said on this subject. We are in a business of relentless repetition, or at least that is our goal: that our repeat business will occur over and over again.

As there *should* be more said, there *will* be as new levels are achieved, maintained and improved again.

Chapter12: The Last Chapter: Satisfaction: EGP Factors:

12-Exist: Realize that there is no one top level.

12-Grow: Identify as often as possible the next level you are going for.

12-Prosper: You must not be satisfied where you are to be able to keep doing what you are doing and prosper.

E(exist) G(grow) P(prosper) List

[Note: at the end of each chapter, there is the "EGP" factor list given as a quick reference list on what to take from that particular chapter to help you first **E**xist, then **G**row, and finally **P**rosper. These are the different levels I strive to achieve in my restaurant. At the end of this book are the 36 points of the EGP factor that will be a good list to refer to as quick reminders to aid in any restaurant operation.]

EGP factors:

Chapter 1: Employees
1-Exist: You must have staff.
1-Grow: Raise your employees' abilities.
1-Prosper: Identify the future leaders quickly and exploit their talent.

Chapter 2: Schedules
2-Exist: You must have staff.
2-Grow: You learn the capabilities of your best people.
2-Prosper: You exploit the capabilities of your best people.

Chapter 3: Situations
3-Exist: Realize that things will not go exactly as planned.
3-Grow: Always work on contingency plans based on past experiences.
3-Prosper: From the very beginning of each shift "go with the punches" in order to avoid distractions.

Chapter 4: Time Robbers
4-Exist: Realize that things will happen to you to disrupt your schedule
4-Grow: Plan on interruptions and allow time for them in your schedule.
4-Prosper: Look at your planned day and anticipate what will be your distractions and try to eliminate them.

Chapter 5: Achievement

5-Exist: Work to develop yourself and staff daily.

5-Grow: Realize that you and your staff can make a difference and achieve a higher level of greatness.

5-Prosper: Using your past achievements to succeed in the future is the way to approach your work.

Chapter 6: Discipline, Development, and Dependability

6-Exist: Surround yourself with dependable people.

6-Grow: Motivate your staff by showing them how you discipline yourself to complete tasks.

6-Prosper: Identify individuals who show potential and aid them in their development to be what they can be.

Chapter 7: Competition

7-Exist: Competition is a must in every society.

7-Grow: Your competition makes you better.

7-Prosper: Compete with yourself to consistently beat your previous best performance.

Chapter 8: Consistency

8-Exist: Do your job the right way, everyday.

8-Grow: Realize that you are being watched and emulated at all times.

8-Prosper: Watch for emerging consistent skills in your staff to see future leaders.

Chapter 9: Interviewing

9-Exist: Do not do "warm body hiring".

9-Grow: Be consistent in questioning and standards.

9-Prosper: Ask yourself, "would I want this person working for my competition?"

Chapter 10: Musings

10-Exist: See what others have to offer.

10-Grow: Learn from others.

10-Prosper: Realize that you are achieving great things and that others learn from you.

Chapter 11: Formula for Achievement

11-Exist: Use what you have experienced to guide you.

11-Grow: Always glean experiences from others.

11-Prosper: Never stop rising to the next level.

Chapter12: The Last Chapter: Satisfaction

12-Exist: Realize that there is no one top level.

12-Grow: Identify as often as possible the next level you are going for.

12-Prosper: You must be satisfied where you are to be able to keep doing what you are doing and prosper.

ABOUT THE AUTHOR

A career spanning over 20 years in the restaurant, during critical developing times for restaurants, George Hearing captures the essence of CORE management directives and objectives. His insightful motivational and sometimes entertaining words are sure to inspire anyone in restaurant management, those pursing such an endeavor, and anyone in the hospitality industry.

He is a disciple of many business writers and he thoughtfully intertwines many different philosophies into his style, he shares his secrets within.